P9-CLS-855

Carey Price

*How a First Nations kid
became a superstar goaltender*

Catherine Rondina

James Lorimer & Company Ltd., Publishers
Toronto

Copyright © 2018 by Catherine Rondina
Published in Canada in 2018. Published in the United States in 2018.

All rights reserved. No part of this book may be reproduced or transmitted in any form or by any means, electronic or mechanical, including photocopying, or by any information storage or retrieval system, without permission in writing from the publisher.

James Lorimer & Company Ltd., Publishers acknowledges funding support from the Ontario Arts Council (OAC), an agency of the Government of Ontario. We acknowledge the support of the Canada Council for the Arts, which last year invested $153 million to bring the arts to Canadians throughout the country. This project has been made possible in part by the Government of Canada and with the support of the Ontario Media Development Corporation.

Cover design: Tyler Cleroux
Cover images: Anita Madsen & Jim Balfe courtesy of Anahim Lake Resort (top), Alamy (bottom)

Library and Archives Canada Cataloguing in Publication

Rondina, Catherine, author
    Carey Price : how a First Nations kid became a superstar goaltender / Catherine Rondina.

(Recordbooks)
Issued in print and electronic formats.
ISBN 978-1-4594-1276-7 (softcover).--ISBN 978-1-4594-1277-4 (EPUB)

    1. Price, Carey, 1987- --Juvenile literature. 2. Hockey goalkeepers--Canada--Biography--Juvenile literature. 3. Native hockey players--Canada--Biography--Juvenile literature. 4. Hockey players--Canada--Biography--Juvenile literature. I. Title. II. Series: Record books

GV848.5.P74R65 2018   j796.962092   C2017-906495-9
                                                         C2017-906496-7

Published by:
James Lorimer & Company Ltd., Publishers
117 Peter Street, Suite 304
Toronto, ON, Canada
M5V 0M3
www.lorimer.ca

Distributed in Canada by:
Formac Lorimer Books
5502 Atlantic Street
Halifax, NS, Canada
B3H 1G4

Distributed in the US by:
Lerner Publisher Services
1251 Washington Ave. N.
Minneapolis, MN, USA
55401
www.lernerbooks.com

Printed and bound in Canada.
Manufactured by Friesens Corporation in Altona, Manitoba, Canada in December 2017.
Job # 239687

*For my sons, Jude and Matthew;
both hockey goaltenders who know it
takes strong spirit and heart plus skill
to play the toughest position in sport.*

In memory of Sheila Barry.

Advanced Praise

"I enjoyed reading this story about Carey tremendously. I'm so proud that he truly believes in his cultural background and where he comes from. He helps our younger generations to see a path in front of them to become successful and famous like him."

— Janie Jack, Culture and Language Teacher —
Anahim Lake School

"A great read for anyone who loves Canada's game and wants to learn more about a great Canadian goalie."

— Bob Nicholson, former President & CEO of
Hockey Canada, Current CEO & Vice-Chairman
of the Edmonton Oilers

Contents

Prologue

Canadians love hockey. It's their game.

It is February 23, 2014, and many Canadians sit glued to their TV sets. Fans across the country are nervous and excited about a crucial hockey game. The Canadian Men's Hockey Team is playing at the Winter Olympic Games in Sochi, Russia. The series has been thrilling to watch. Team Canada is undefeated at these Olympics. The country is going hockey crazy!

Every player on the team is feeling the pressure. They want to make their country proud. They're here to get the job done. Today Team Canada is playing for the gold medal against Team Sweden. Both teams want to prove that they are the best hockey team in the world.

The players feel great support from the fans. The arena is filled with cheering people. The Canadian fans are dressed in red and white. Some have painted their faces red and white, too. Hundreds of Maple Leaf flags are waving in the crowd. The air feels like it is filled with electricity.

In net for Team Canada is 26-year-old goaltender Carey Price. Carey is proud to be representing his country. The pressure can be overwhelming. A lot is riding on this game — a whole country's pride in the game they call their own. But Carey can handle it. He has been Team Canada's goalie through the whole series. Carey has not lost a single game for his team. He has stopped shots from some of the best players in the world.

Carey stands tall and proud in the net. With his stick in his right hand, his catcher in his left, he stays focused. Carey's eyes never leave the puck.

Many people think that Sweden is the better team. But Carey has been playing some of his best hockey during these Olympic games. He thinks with great pride about where he has come from and how far he has gone. His teammates are in front of him and his country is behind him. Carey is determined to bring the gold medal home for Canada.

1 A Simpler Life

About 850 kilometres north of Vancouver, British Columbia, is a small town called Anahim Lake. The population is about 360, mostly First Nations people. Another 729 people live on the Ulkatcho First Nations reserve nearby. Anahim Lake is surrounded by snow-covered mountains, lots of lakes and wide-open spaces. It was the perfect place to grow up. And one boy who loved nature and spent most of his

Anahim Lake

time outdoors did grow up there. This tiny perfect town was home to NHL superstar goalie Carey Price.

Carey was born in Vancouver, British Columbia, on August 16, 1987. His parents, Jerry and Lynda, wanted a simpler life for their young family. So, they moved back to Lynda's hometown of Anahim Lake when Carey was a toddler. Anahim Lake is made up of a village and the Ulkatcho First Nation reserve. Carey's family did not live on the reserve, but Carey's mother's family were Ulkatcho First Nation. It was important to Lynda that Carey and his sister know the proud heritage of their indigenous ancestors. Anahim Lake was a small, close community, and Lynda had many relatives and friends there. Lynda's family were ranchers and hunting guides, who knew and respected the land. Lynda Price knew how important it was to share her culture with her children. Lynda's four brothers, Mike, Larry, Gary and David and her mother, Theresa, passed along their family history and helped keep Carey connected to his ancestors.

First Peoples

First Nations is the term used to describe some of the Indigenous peoples of Canada. British Columbia has the largest number of First Nations communities in Canada. The Ulkatcho First Nation people are part of the Carrier First Nation ethnic group. The Ulkatcho speak Dakelh language. The region they live in is called Cariboo-Chilcotin.

Carey's father Jerry was born in Coronation, Alberta. Jerry's family was made up of farmers and ranchers, like Lynda's. They loved the land and worked hard. Hockey was also a big part of their lives. As a young boy, Jerry liked to play hockey. His favourite position was in net, stopping pucks. Jerry became a pretty good goalie and played Junior hockey in the Western Hockey League (WHL). In 1978, he was drafted by the Philadelphia Flyers to play in the National Hockey League

Anahim Lake School's symbol is a cowboy riding rodeo style.

(NHL). But Jerry never did get a chance to play a game in the NHL. Like many young hockey players selected by NHL teams, Jerry was never called up to play in the major leagues. Jerry did play four seasons as a professional player on other non-NHL teams. He decided to retire from hockey in 1983.

When Jerry and Lynda decided to start a family together, they knew that moving back to Anahim Lake was a good idea. The Price family loved the simple life they could have there. Their home was built out of wooden logs and had a tin roof. Carey's little sister Kayla and his *Atsoo* (Grandmother) Theresa, Lynda's mother, lived there too. The house was built on their 35 acres of land. A creek ran right outside their back door. Corkscrew Creek would become a very important part of Carey's life as a young boy.

Home Sweet Home

Carey loved growing up in Anahim Lake. He listed some of the special things about it on the Montreal Canadiens' website, such as McLean's General Store, where you could find anything you wanted. The great fishing you can do there. Playing hockey on the frozen pond. Carey especially loved his mom's cooking. And bannock, a fried bread that is a staple in Indigenous meals.

Painting of the original Anahim Lake School building where Carey went to school.

"We have pictures of him when he was barely able to walk. His mother and me out on the creek, holding him up. Or dragging him around in a little sleigh," recalls Jerry Price, in a *New York Times* interview. "So he spent a lot of time just being on the ice." By the time Carey was two years old, he was learning to skate. Jerry was the perfect teacher, coaching his son and showing him all he knew and loved about being on the ice.

From the time he was very young, Carey loved the outdoors. The Price family spent a lot of time doing things together as a family. Carey and his dad would fish together for hours. Carey remembers his dad telling him about the first time Carey caught a fish. He said Carey was about three years old. Carey got a little scared when the fish was hooked on his line. He didn't know what was going on, so he threw his fishing pole into the water! In a video that shows him fishing with angler Ben Woo, Carey says that some of his best memories are of being out on the lake in a little aluminum boat, fishing with his dad.

Throughout his early childhood Carey loved animals. His family home always had pets. Carey especially liked dogs and horses. He also learned to ride horses as a very young boy. There were always animals around for Carey to take care of. He spent many happy hours playing with the family pets and watching the woodland creatures that lived on their property.

It seemed that Jerry and Lynda had made the right choice for their family. Anahim Lake was an ideal place for a young boy to grow up. There was fresh air and lots of room to dream big.

2 Skates, School and Family Ties

As Carey grew, so did his love of skating and playing hockey. His dad Jerry was always happy to share his love of the game. Every winter, as the air turned colder, Jerry would build a rink on the creek. He would shovel snow off a portion of the ice. Then he would drill a hole to pump water from under the ice to flood the surface and keep it smooth. He even put up floodlights so that they could keep skating after it got dark. Carey and his dad would often take turns in the net, taking shots on each other. "My dad showed me a lot," Carey told Sportsnet reporter Arden Zwelling, "There's lessons he taught me at an early age that I still use today."

NHLers Who Learned to Skate on Backyard Rinks and Frozen Ponds

(Just like Carey!)

Wayne Gretzky, Gordie Howe, Ryan Getzlaf, Jonathan Quick, Ben Lovejoy, Corey Perry, Jordan Nolan, Teemu Selanne, Mathieu Perreault

Carey's mom Lynda remembers Carey coming home after school and skating until dinnertime. After dinner, he'd go back out on the ice until it was time to get ready for bed. Every chance they got,

Carey's class photo from the 1995–1996 school year.
Carey is circled in the top row.

Carey and his friends would play hockey
on Jerry's homemade rink. They'd skate
laps, take shots and play shinny. No one
really kept score. Most of the players
didn't wear any hockey gear. But when
Carey was in net he always wore the
goalie mask his dad had made for him.

If none of Carey's buddies were around
to play, Carey would put his little sister

Kayla in net. Kayla often didn't have any equipment on, just a stick in her hand. "He was taking light shots at me and I had his stick at a tilt, so the blade was aimed right for my nose," Kayla told a Kamloops newspaper. "The puck shot off the blade and hit me straight in the nose." After they had stopped Kayla's nosebleed, they decided her goaltending days were over. Carey was the one with the talent. He was going to be the goalie in the family!

Canada's Game

Canadians have a long history of playing pond hockey. The Bank of Canada decided to recognize that. Between 2002 and 2013, the back of the Canadian five-dollar bill showed an illustration of four kids playing hockey on an outdoor rink.

Even with all his time on the ice, Carey had school to think about, too.

Carey was a good student. He went to Anahim Lake School, where he had a lot of friends. Carey is still friends with many of the kids he went to school with. School secretary Dianne Chamberlain remembers Carey as a quiet student who did well in school. She recalls he was good at any sport he tried. Carey was a natural athlete and played soccer, basketball and lacrosse. Anahim Lake School had an outdoor rink for Carey and his friends to skate on.

One year, Dianne Chamberlain was the computer teacher at Anahim Lake School. She asked her students to put together a very special book. The book was called "Remembering Moments in Time . . . Our Elders." Each student was asked to write a story about someone they admired in their lives. Carey's story was about his Atsoo (grandmother) Theresa. Carey wrote about her family and what life was

Anahim Lake School banner celebrating the 2nd place win of the Floor Hockey Team in 1998. Carey and the team signed the banner.

like for her as a child. He told how, as a young girl, she had to gather wood, chase the milking cow and keep the house clean for her family. Theresa also had to help care for her brothers and sisters. She had many responsibilities as a child.

Carey had great respect for his grandmother. He was impressed that her family lived off the land. Carey also wrote about the special moments he got to spend with his grandmother as they fished, swam, rode horses and did beadwork together. Theresa taught Carey how important and special his family's heritage was.

When Carey wasn't playing hockey, he loved watching it. His favourite team growing up was the Edmonton Oilers. Of course, Carey kept an eye on the hottest goaltenders in the NHL at the time. Marty Turco and Patrick Roy were his on-ice heroes. Marty Turco was great at handling the puck. Patrick Roy was an incredible goalie who was famous for his butterfly style in net. He could stop shots with his legs outstretched, like butterfly wings. Carey learned a lot about netminding from studying what his heroes did.

Also among Carey's hockey heroes were his relatives. Shane Doan, the former captain of the Arizona Coyotes, is a cousin on his dad's side. Carey was just eight years old when Shane made it to the NHL. "He's a great guy," said Carey about Shane in an NHL.com interview. "I always looked up to him when I was growing up." Pro hockey players Keaton Ellerby and Brett Scheffelmaier are also related to the Price family. "Shane and Brett were big role models for Carey," said Jerry Price during an NHL.com interview. "Their playing at a high level made it seem more attainable."

But the family member who influenced Carey most was his dad. Jerry often coached the teams Carey was on. "I just wanted Carey to have an opportunity to play the game that meant so much to me and that I enjoyed so much," Jerry said to *New York Times* reporters Jeff Klein and Stu Hackel. "I wanted to try to help him develop some skills that may or may not ever amount to anything. Just a dad enjoying time with his son."

The Family Way — Some Fathers, Sons and Grandsons in the NHL

The Apps: Syl (father); Syl Jr. (son)

The Bouchards: Émile (father); Pierre (son)

The Domis: Tie (father); Max (son)

The Folignos: Mike (father); Nick (son), Marcus (son)

The Hextalls: Bryan Sr. (father); Bryan Jr. (son), Dennis (son); Ron (grandson)

The Howes: Gordie (father); Mark (son), Marty (son)

The Hulls: Bobby (father); Brett (son)

The Parisés: J.P. (father); Zach (son)

The Patricks: Lester (father); Lynn (son), Muzz (son); Craig (grandson), Glenn (grandson)

The Stastnys: Peter (father); Paul (son), Yan (son)

The Sutters: Brent (father); Brandon (son)

The Nolans: Ted (father); Brandon (son), Jordan (son)

3 Up, Up, and Away!

By the time Carey was 9, he was becoming very skilled at hockey. It was becoming clear that Carey had something special. And he was willing to work hard at it. Carey had discovered that he belonged in the net. He loved being a difference-maker in the game. Even more importantly, he was getting really good at it!

Every winter, Carey skated on a frozen creek. A rink was made by shoveling snow off the icy surface. It had snowbanks rolled in chicken wire for its sideboards. From December to March, in temperatures as low as -30° Celsius, Carey practiced his hockey skills. Carey's mother Lynda said that playing hockey with the older boys helped make him a better player.

> ## Other names for goalies
>
> goaltender, netminder, netkeeper, goalkeeper, tender, tendy, keeper

But Jerry knew that for Carey to really learn the game, he needed to play on a team. Most kids Carey's age were already playing league hockey. The problem was that Anahim Lake didn't have any organized teams for Carey to play on. They didn't even have an indoor hockey arena!

Playing Net Wasn't His First Choice

Carey is one of the best goalie puck handlers in the league. He says he learned how to handle the puck as a defenceman when he first started playing hockey. In the end, Carey liked saving pucks more than scoring goals with them. But he still has a wicked shot from the blue line!

Jerry contacted the nearest town with a house league team. He signed Carey up to play. There was just one small problem. That town was Williams Lake and it took 3 hours to drive there! Jerry would pick Carey up right after school to get him to his 6:00 p.m. practice on time. Carey and Jerry would have to travel 3 hours to get to Williams Lake and then drive 3 more hours to get back home to Anahim Lake. But Jerry felt his son deserved a chance to play on a team. He was determined to give Carey that chance.

Soon Jerry and Carey had to drive the 640-kilometre round trip to Williams Lake and back a couple of times a week. "Much of the drive was along quiet country roads, through wilderness country. We took a few spins in the ditch," recalls Carey in a *New York Times* interview.

It was a long way to go. Carey often did his homework or slept during the drive. Carey said that he would fall asleep dreaming of the day he might play in the NHL. "It was a lot of traveling, but it was time well spent," Jerry Price told a *Globe and Mail* newspaper reporter. "We got to spend a lot of time together." Jerry says that they spent many winter nights driving home listening to hockey games on the car radio.

Carey did so well his first year in house league that he was asked to join the traveling team. The team would play teams from other towns. This meant

The Williams Lake Minor Hockey Association logo from Carey's minor hockey days.

having to be in Williams Lake even more. Carey had to be there for two practices a week, plus games. Jerry had his pilot's license, and he decided to buy a small plane. The plane was a four-seat Piper Cherokee. "It was more of a lawnmower with wings," Jerry joked in a *Globe and Mail* interview. But flying cut the 3-hour trip down to just 45 minutes.

Carcy even learned to fly his dad's plane. "I learned to fly at a young age so

A Piper Cherokee 4-seater plane like the one Jerry flew to get Carey to his minor hockey league games and practices.

I got a little extra out of it," Carey said in the same interview. "You've just got to keep it in a straight line and go over that mountain. The wind blows you every which way, but you just keep her steady."

Carey playing hockey took a lot of time and was a great expense for the family. Jerry and Lynda had to be sure that Carey really wanted to play. Jerry says that the idea of playing any sport is to have fun. He always tried to make sure Carey was having fun. "That's why they call it a game," explains Jerry to habseyesontheprize.com. "It's to have fun." Jerry says that his son made the decision on his own. Jerry and Lynda were never pushy hockey parents. Jerry would often ask Carey if he was happy playing the game. He never forced Carey to play. "He liked to play and I wanted to give him the chance to play if that's what he wanted to do. Because I know how important hockey was to me in my life," Jerry told *Canadian Press* journalist Donna Spencer.

Carey was always very confident as a child. He believed in himself. Jerry thought that Carey's confidence came from Lynda, who was a strong and confident leader in her community. "I just think he had made up his mind as a young person that this is what he was going to be," Jerry said in an interview with Canadiens.com. "He just never doubted it."

As long as Carey said he wanted to keep playing, his mom and dad would be there to support him. They knew that their son was a talented athlete and that hockey was important to him. Eventually, Carey and his family moved to Williams Lake so that Carey could play minor hockey and finish high school.

Hockey in Williams Lake

Carey was 9 years old when he joined the Williams Lake Minor Hockey Association. He played his whole minor career there until he was 15. In Carey's final season he played with the Williams Lake Midget AAA Timberwolves and helped them win the British Columbia provincial championship title. Carey also played on Team North in 2002 at the BC Winter Games in Williams Lake.

4 Leaving Home to Follow a Dream

By 2002, Carey was one of the top amateur goalies in Canada. Many people in the hockey world were talking about his goaltending skills and style. At 15 years old, it was time for Carey to move up again in the game of hockey. This meant taking the next step toward making his dream of playing pro hockey come true. Carey and his family knew this meant he would have to leave home.

Carey's talent in the net got him noticed

by the world's top amateur league. The Canadian Hockey League (CHL) is where the best junior hockey players go to develop their game. More than 60 CHL teams in western Canada and the northwest United States make up the Western Hockey League (WHL). The team that drafted Carey was the Tri-City Americans of the WHL.

Carey was the first netminder to be chosen in the draft. He was picked seventh overall. Being selected in the top 10 picks is very good for a goalie! The team was based in Kennewick, in the state of Washington. It was a big city. Home to more than 60,000 people, it was very different from Carey's hometown of Anahim Lake. Carey was very excited, and probably nervous. But he understood that he had to leave his home, his family and Canada to make his hockey dream a reality.

When young hockey players are drafted and have to move away from home, they often live with families who billet players for the team. These families open their homes to teenage players. They give them a place to stay and the chance to live as a part of a family in their new city.

Carey went to live in Pasco, part of the Tri-City area, with Dennis and Jill Williams. Over the years, they had offered their home to many young hockey players. Carey said that the Williams family became his "second family." Jill and Dennis welcomed him into their home and took care of him. Jill and Dennis said Carey was very quiet and took some time to adjust to his new life in a city. But like any of the teenagers who stayed with the Williams family, Carey was a typical boy. Jill says that Carey would eat anything she put in front of him. "Carey was the biggest eater I've ever had," Jill told a Sportsnet reporter. "He could put down a couple of steaks and a few twice-baked potatoes in one sitting."

Carey wearing Tri-City Americans jersey, 2004.

Food for Thought

Like most young athletes Carey always had a big appetite. Anyone who plays sports needs to properly nourish their bodies to stay strong and healthy. Carey's favourite meal is his mom's homemade lasagna. Carey doesn't cook a lot himself, but you can see him having fun cooking on YouTube.

Carey did a lot of things with the Williams family that he did with his own. Dennis and Carey would fish and hunt together. Dennis told Sportsnet reporter Arden Zwelling that Carey was "a natural." For Carey, it was much like being home, spending time with his dad. It helped Carey get used to his new life away from his family.

The other sport that Carey continued to practice when he wasn't playing hockey was rodeo roping. Carey loved the rodeo! He had grown up with horses in Anahim Lake and learned to ride when he was

The logo for Carey's Junior hockey team, the Tri-City Americans.

very young. But it was during his years in Williams Lake that he got hooked on lassoing. He got to be pretty good with his rope tricks. Jill Williams recalls that Carey would sit on the couch, watching TV and twirling a lasso at his feet. He even lassoed her once as she was coming through the living room with a basket of laundry! Even today Carey still loves rodeo roping. When asked what he would have done if he hadn't made it to the NHL, Carey says he would have joined the rodeo.

A Cowboy at Heart

"Hockey has always been my first love and I couldn't wait for the lake to freeze every winter, but as a kid I always had a cowboy hat on and my toy six shooters in each hand," recalled Price in an NHL.com interview. "I must've worn that stuff everywhere until I was like eight or nine." He still does competitive roping at rodeos every summer during the off-season. He's been known to have a lariat in the team dressing room. He likes to joke around, using the rope to lasso his teammates.

Besides having fun with the Williams family, Carey had hockey to think about. His first game with the Tri-City Americans was during the 2002–2003 season. But Carey would only get to play that one game. In his second season with the Tri-City

Americans, Carey was the backup goalie for Tyler Weiman, drafted by the Colorado Avalanche. Carey got to play 28 games in net that year. At first, all Carey got to do was sit on the bench and open the gate for his teammates going off and onto the ice. The Williams family gave Carey a can of WD-40 for Christmas his first year with the team, joking that he needed the oil to keep the gate working well. But Tyler Weiman wasn't playing well as the season progressed. The coach, Don Nachbaur, decided to give Carey a chance to show what he could do.

The next season Carey took over the position and proved himself as the top goaltender. The 63 games he played was a league record for the most games played in the WHL by a goalie. Coach Nachbaur told Sportsnet, "It was obvious that Carey was gonna be our guy. He was 16 years old and he was outplaying a guy who was on his way to the NHL."

Carey in net, October 15, 2004: Tri-City Americans vs. Prince George Cougars.

Whenever the Tri-City Americans were playing near Anahim Lake, in Kamloops or Prince George, Carey's friends and family came to see him. Relatives and friends would climb into their cars and make the long drive to see their hometown hero play.

5 Steady Between the Pipes

Carey was becoming a hockey superstar at the Junior level. For young players, playing Junior hockey is like being in a high-level competition. It's where you begin to play against the best players in the game. And that means you improve as a player too. Every player on the ice is after one thing — a contract to play in the big leagues. It can be very competitive, but Carey was ready for the challenge.

Junior players have to play their very

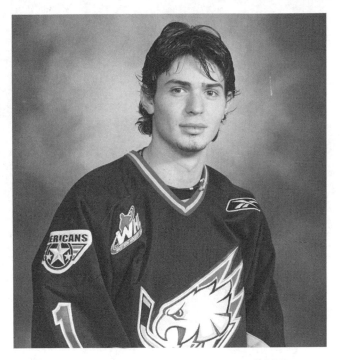

Carey in his Tri-City Americans jersey, 2005.

best. Hockey scouts begin to look for players in the Junior leagues. The scouts are paid to look for the most talented players. They want to take the best players to play on pro teams and maybe, one day, to the NHL. One thing that scouts rely on is the scouting reports kept on each player that record how the athlete is performing. Most of these reports are about a player's numbers. For a goalie like Carey, it's all about his numbers when he's in net, between the pipes. How many wins has he had? How many shots has he stopped? What is his save percent average? Carey was one of the best in his league. He had great numbers!

In his hockey career with the Tri-City Americans, Carey made team history. He posted a record 83 wins with a 2.53 goals-against average. Those 83 wins gave him the third-best record in Tri-City Americans franchise history. Carey had 15 career shutouts, the best of any goalie in the franchise, with a save percentage of .915.

Playing the goalie position on a team is very stressful. The one thing that many people noticed about Carey was how relaxed he seemed in the net. Tri-City

Another logo of the Tri-City Americans.

Americans Coach Nachbaur said Carey made it look easy. During team practices, Carey would stand in his net and look bored. He would kick out a puck with his pad. Or he would use his blocker to stop a shot. The players couldn't score on him. But he made it look like he wasn't working very hard. According to a Sportsnet.ca reporter, Coach Nachbaur once yelled to Carey, "Would you start trying?" Carey replied, "Coach, I know where all these shots are going. It's too easy."

Carey in net, January 6, 2006: Tri-City Americans vs. Portland Winterhawks.

Some people saw how relaxed Carey was and wondered if he didn't practice enough. But Carey did work hard. He trained every day. The players who tried to score on him could tell. He was really good. It was just that he made stopping the puck look easy. Carey could follow the puck with his eyes anywhere on the ice. Keeping an eye on it. Never letting it out of his sight. This skill is much like when Carey would watch wild game while hunting with his father back home in British Columbia.

Carey thinks that he gets his relaxed style from his dad. Jerry was always easy-going and a patient teacher. "Carey's always been calm like that, even when we were little," said his cousin, Keaton Ellerby, a former NHL defenseman, who now plays pro hockey in Sweden. Keaton said in an interview with the *Globe and Mail* that "it might be because Carey grew up in the middle of nowhere." Carey said, "There's not a lot to get excited about. And I think a lot of it comes from my parents and the way they raised me."

Carey's Junior years were full of great highlights. His calmness and confidence helped get him and his Tri-City Americans through five seasons. He set team records, won awards and eventually met the girl of his dreams.

Hockey was becoming an even bigger part of Carey's life, but he still had some time for friends and dating. Carey met a girl named Angela Webber while living in Pasco. Angela remembers that their first date was all about hockey, of course. They went to a restaurant after one of Carey's games. Carey invited Angela to come and see him play the next night. The night Angela came to watch him play, Carey had an awful game. He let in eight goals and was pulled from the net! But Carey didn't think Angela was the reason he had bad luck that night. He and Angela began to date.

Some Indigenous NHL Players

Past: George Armstrong, Jonathan Cheechoo, Theo Fleury, Cody McCormick, Wade Redden, Sheldon Souray, Bryan Trottier

Present: Rene Bourque, Micheal Ferland, Vern Fiddler, Dwight King, Jordan Nolan, T.J. Oshie, Jordin Tootoo

6 Playing for Canada

Carey's impressive play in the net made him a natural choice when it came to picking players to represent Canada. Carey was always considered for teams when Canada needed a goaltender. He has played for Canada in the IIHF World Championships, the Olympics and the World Cup of Hockey.

In the 2003–2004 season Carey made his first international hockey debut at the IIHF (International Ice Hockey

Federation) Ice Hockey Under-18 World Championship. For the first time in his hockey career, Carey wore Canada's maple leaf on his jersey. Teams from around the world were there to compete for gold. Soon after that, at the age of 16, Carey played on one of 5 teams representing Canada at the 2004 World Under-17 Hockey Challenge. The series was held in St. John's, Newfoundland, and Carey's team took home the silver medal for Canada.

Carey's junior hockey career had made him a goalie to be noticed. He had grown into a strong young man. His large body filled the net. Carey was a physical threat in goal. Players shooting on Carey looked for an open space to shoot the puck through and score. Carey's size and skill didn't leave much room for that!

Goalie Language

W – Win – games the goaltender has won

L – Loss – games the goaltender has lost

T – Tie – games the goaltender has tied

SO – Shutout – a game where a goalie has had no goals scored against him

SOG – Shots On Goal – total number of shots the goalie has had on him during a game

Carey was on the ice twice in 2005 representing his country. In April, he was part of the Canadian team who took home gold in the IIHF Under-18 World Championship in the Czech Republic. In the summer of 2005, Carey was in net for Team Canada again. This time the Under-18 team played in the Ivan Hlinka Memorial World Cup in the Czech Republic. They won the silver medal for Canada.

In December of 2006, Carey was off to

the 2006–2007 World Junior Championship in Leksand, Sweden. Once again, he proudly wore the maple leaf for Canada. His family were in the stands, cheering on Carey and Team Canada. Canada had a hard-fought win against the USA in the semi-final game. The winner had to be decided in a shootout. After the game Carey was out of breath. He told a reporter from HockeysFuture.com that he was tired, excited and filled with mixed emotions.

Team Canada would go on to win the gold medal at the championship. Carey was "running down a dream that he has had since he was a child," his mother Lynda told reporter Terry Koshan from canoe.com. She was proud and happy for him. So were all his friends and family back home in Anahim Lake. "I'm proud of who I am and where I came from, and being from such a small community," Carey said in the same interview.

7 The NHL Takes Notice

Carey's hard work and determination were paying off. He was considered one of the top young goalies in North America. The scouts were impressed with his talent in the net. Many pro teams were interested in having a goalie like Carey play for them.

In 2005, the NHL Entry Draft was in Ottawa, Ontario. It was a big event for hockey fans that year. Everyone was excited about a young player from Cole Harbour,

Nova Scotia. The player's name was Sidney Crosby. People who knew hockey thought Crosby was going to be a superstar one day. He was the player everyone wanted. It was Pittsburgh that got the first pick that year, and they chose Sidney for the Penguins.

At that same draft, Carey was sitting at a table waiting for his name to be called. Carey's family was there to support him. He felt nervous and excited at the same time. It was big day for the whole family. Carey's dream was coming true.

Four picks after Sidney Crosby, the Montreal Canadiens management group went to the microphone and Trevor Timmins announced their selection. "*Le Club de Hockey Canadiens est fier de selectionner* — the Montreal Canadiens are proud to select — from the WHL Tri-City Americans, goaltender Carey Price."

Carey stood up from the table. There was a slight smile and a look of surprise on his

*A Habs fan's goalie mask signed by Carey Price,
from his first year with the Canadiens.*

face. No one, not even Carey, had expected
that he would be drafted this high. Carey
hugged his mom, sister Kayla and his dad.
Then he walked to the stage to be given his
Montreal Canadiens jersey and hat.

The Canadiens selected Carey fifth overall. Carey was the first goaltender to be selected at the draft. This meant that the Montreal Canadiens considered him to be the top goaltender available. It was a very proud moment for Carey and his family. All their hard work had been worth it. Carey would be playing for one of the greatest teams in hockey history. Carey was just as amazed as anyone at being picked fifth. "I wasn't expecting to go this high, but I'll take it," Carey told a TSN reporter.

Even though Carey was selected by the Montreal Canadiens, there was still lots of work to be done with his current team. Young, drafted players must finish off the season with their Junior team. Most players continue to play in lower level leagues until their NHL coaches feel they are ready for major league play.

Carey returned to play the 2006–2007 season with the Tri-City Americans. It was his best season with the team. Carey won the Del Wilson Trophy as the best goaltender in the WHL and the 2007 Canadian Major Junior Goaltender of the Year award. Carey's record that season was 30–13–1, for wins, losses and ties. In the same season, Carey was also chosen for the WHL West First All-Star Team and the Canadian Major Junior First All-Star Team.

Carey helped take his team to the first round of the WHL playoffs. The series was against the Seattle Thunderbirds, who knocked the Tri-City Americans out in the first round. But Carey's hockey season wasn't quite over yet.

Making Hockey History

Carey is the only goaltender to win the Jack A. Butterfield Trophy, the World Junior Championship MVP and the CHL Goaltender of the Year Award all in the same year.

The Montreal Canadiens sent Carey to play with their top farm team, the Hamilton Bulldogs. All major sports teams have farm teams. Younger players are sent to a farm team to get experience and training. It's where they prepare to play in the big leagues. The Bulldogs were part of the American Hockey League (AHL), and were just finishing off their regular season. Carey played the final two games in net for the Bulldogs. He allowed only three goals in the two games he played. The Bulldogs then moved on to the 2007 American League playoffs for the Calder Cup. And Carey went with them.

For the Calder Cup, 16 teams play off in multiple best-of-seven series. The Calder Cup playoff was a total of just 22 games for the Bulldogs. In the conference finals Carey and the Bulldogs played the Hershey Bears. In Game 1 Carey was outstanding. He made 46 saves and earned a shutout. In Game 2 the Bears came back to win by a score of 4–2. Game 3 saw the Bulldogs take advantage of six power play chances to win the game 5–2. In Game 4 the Bulldogs were in control from the start of the game, and won with a 6–2 victory. The Bulldogs took Game 5 and the series in front of a cheering hometown crowd. They defeated the Hershey Bears 2–1. The Bulldogs had won the series 4 games to 1 to win the Calder Cup for the first time in their team's history!

Carey was as solid as a wall in the net. His Goals Against Average (GAA) was 2.06 and he had a save percentage of .936. Carey also had two shutouts during the playoffs. He was awarded the Jack A. Butterfield Trophy as the series MVP. At just 19 years old, Carey was the youngest player to ever win it.

Lynda Price Makes Her Own History

In 2007 Carey's mom Lynda was elected chief of the Ulkatcho First Nation. Lynda Price was the first woman to be elected to the position. Carey is very proud of his mother. He sees Lynda as a hardworking, confident leader who is passionate about her heritage. Jerry Price said this in an interview for NHL.com/canadiens/news.

8 Bonjour Montreal!

In 2007, Carey officially began his pro hockey career. His name was added to the Montreal Canadiens team roster. He was just 20 years old and playing in the NHL. Carey's dream had come true!

The Montreal Canadiens, or the Habs, as their fans call them, are one of the toughest hockey teams in the world to play for. They won their first Stanley Cup in 1916. They went on to win more Stanley Cups than any other team in the NHL.

The letter "H" for Habitants?

Many Canadiens fans call their team the "Habs" or "Les Habs," short or for "Habitants" meaning farmers from the countryside. It was a nickname given to them by their original owner back in 1909. Some believe the "H" on the Canadiens jersey stands for Habitants. But the team was originally called the Club de Hockey Canadien, meaning Canadian Hockey Club. The "H" in the logo is for "hockey."

Playing for a team like Montreal can be a lot of pressure. Being part of a very successful hockey club puts a lot of strain on the players to maintain that record. It can be very stressful. Habs fans love their team and they know a lot about hockey. Every player and every game is talked about in the news in the hockey-crazy city of Montreal.

Playing goal for this famous team meant a lot of demands would be put on Carey.

Montreal was one of the Original Six teams that first made up the NHL. A 1934–1935 hockey program from the Montreal Forum.

Montreal fans proudly display the Go Habs Go flag before the puck drops at the Bell Centre for the February 23, 2017 game against the New York Islanders.

Montreal fans can be tough. Carey told NHL.com in an interview how difficult it can be to play in Montreal. "When you're winning here there's no better place to play," explained Carey. "But when you're not playing well here it's definitely tough."

The wall of the Montreal Canadiens dressing room at the Bell Centre had a message for its players — "Pas d'Excuses."

This means "no excuses" and that's what it takes to play on this team. The dressing room also has a list of all the names of great players who were once Montreal Canadiens. One of the longest lists is of past Montreal goalies who have won the Vezina Trophy. The Vezina is awarded to the best NHL goaltender of the year. It was a reminder to Carey of the great goalies who had played on the team before him.

Carey began his rookie year as the backup goalie for the team. He made his first start in net for the Montreal Canadiens on October 10, 2007. The Canadiens were in Pittsburgh to play against the Penguins. The Penguins were a top-scoring team with superstar Sidney Crosby in their lineup. Carey stood tall in the net. The Penguins fired 28 shots at Carey. He stopped 26 of them. Montreal won the game 3–2.

Carey recorded his rookie debut in the NHL with a win!

In his first month with the Habs, Carey was awarded the Canadiens' Molson Cup. This is given to the player with the most first-star-of-the-game selections, as chosen by the sports media, in a month. In Carey's first month with the team, his name had been selected more than any other Montreal player's. He was becoming a favourite of many Montrealers. Carey was proving himself to the hockey fans and the sports media of Montreal.

The 3 Star Selection

The tradition of picking the top 3 players or stars of an NHL hockey game began in 1936. The 3 stars are chosen by the sports media from the hometown team. Three stars are selected in order and their names are announced at the end of the game. Most players come out to skate around the ice and wave to the crowd.

In January, Carey got called back to play with the Hamilton Bulldogs. He played with them for one month and then returned to the Canadiens. In February, Carey got his first NHL career shutout, against the Philadelphia Flyers. Shortly after Carey's shutout, the Canadiens traded their starting goaltender Cristobal Huet. Carey Price was now the Montreal Canadiens' number-one goalie!

Carey took his new starting position very seriously. With Carey in net, the Canadiens finished first in the Eastern Conference. It was the first time they had finished in the top spot in more than 15 years! Carey had finished off the regular season as the best rookie goaltender in the NHL. He had 24 wins and 3 shutouts. His save percentage was .920.

Now it was onto the first round of the Stanley Cup Playoffs. The Canadiens faced an old rival, the Boston Bruins, in the first round. Before a winner could be decided, the series went all the way to a nail-biting Game 7. Boston had won 3 games and Montreal had 3 wins as well. Game 7 would decide the winner. Carey was unbeatable in net. He stopped all 25 shots that the Boston Bruins fired. The Montreal Canadiens won the game 5–0.

But the next round of play against the Philadelphia Flyers wasn't as successful. The Canadiens were defeated by the Flyers. Still, it had been a great first season for Carey. He was named to the NHL's All-Rookie Team to honour his incredible first year as an NHL player.

Carey's first season in the NHL had been very successful. But the loss to the Philadelphia Flyers was tough to take. He said he was not going to look at his goalie equipment for three months. His plan was to hop in his pickup truck and head west. Carey was heading home to think about the loss. But Montreal fans were looking toward the future, not the past. They were pretty excited about what was to come with their young superstar in net.

Original Six

The Montreal Canadiens are one of the Original Six teams, from when the NHL first began. The original six NHL teams were the Montreal Canadiens, the Toronto Maple Leafs, the Detroit Red Wings, the Chicago Blackhawks, the Boston Bruins and the New York Rangers. All six of these teams are still part of the NHL today!

9 Playing Under Pressure

The Montreal Canadiens and their fans were very excited about the 2008–2009 season. Carey was now 21 years old and playing some of his best hockey. The season ahead looked promising. Carey won 7 of the first 10 games he played in net. He even posted a shutout against the Ottawa Senators in November.

Then on December 30, 2008, everything changed. Carey injured his ankle during a game against the Tampa Bay Lightning.

The injury was very serious. It took Carey out of the net for nearly a month. He was in a lot of pain for a long time.

Ouch — That Hurts!

The goalie position in hockey is one of the hardest positions to play of any sport. It's tough on your body and on your mind. Goalies often continue playing even when injured. The most common injuries are to the legs and lower body. The biggest mistake goalies make is to try to play again too soon after they've been hurt.

Even though Carey was injured, the Montreal fans voted for him as the starting goalic for the 2009 NHL All-Star Game. They still believed in him. That meant a lot to Carey. The All-Star Game was to be played in Montreal that year and it would be Carey's first. Carey also played goal for the 2009 NHL Young Stars Game.

But first Carey had to get over his injuries. Carey found it hard to get back on his skates. He had to work hard with his trainers to recover. He struggled to return to the game. His goalie partner was Jaroslav Halak and they had to split the time in net. During the final games of the regular season, the Canadiens lost 20 and only won 7. They still made it into the first round of the playoffs. But the Boston Bruins swept them out of the series. The Canadiens didn't win one game against their rivals. Carey allowed 15 goals in his four games against the Bruins.

Carey's struggles in the net continued into the 2009–2010 season. It was a hard time for him. He was recovering from his injuries and fighting to keep his position. With Halak in net the team was winning. By the end of the season Carey had lost his job as Montreal's starting goalie to Jaroslav Halak. Carey had to sit on the bench and watch his teammates battle it out on the ice. Halak took the team all the way to the Eastern Conference Finals of the Stanley Cup Playoffs. Carey was frustrated by his injuries and just wanted to return to the ice. But Carey didn't play very much during the playoffs. He had only one start in net during the post-season games. And when he was in net, he continued to have difficulties.

The fans were tough on Carey too. They wanted the superstar they had seen in the World Juniors. They wanted the first-round draft pick that everyone had been so excited about. They teased him and called his name, "Ca-rey, Ca-rey!" whenever he made an easy save. One night when he was named one of the three stars of the game, the hometown fans booed him. Carey was feeling the pressure of playing in a hockey town like Montreal.

In just over a year Carey had gone from being considered one of the best goalies in the world to a backup netminder who had to watch the game from the bench.

As the Montreal Canadiens' dream of another Stanley Cup died with the playoff loss, many fans wondered what had happened to Carey. And what would happen to him. Carey and Halak were both free agents at the end of the season. This meant that they were free to leave Montreal and sign to play with another team. Fans and sports reporters all had their opinions. Some people thought keeping Carey was the smart thing to do. Others thought Halak should be the Number 1 goalie for the team.

On June 17, 2010, the team owners made their decision. The Canadiens decided to keep the younger goalie. They traded Halak to the St. Louis Blues. Carey re-signed with Montreal. He was

Carey in net, April 5, 2017 at the KeyBank Center for the Montreal vs. Buffalo Sabres game. Montreal lost 2–1.

given $5.5 million to return to the team for another two years. Many fans were surprised. Some were even angry. Carey was a little surprised too. Even the future Prime Minister Justin Trudeau commented on the trade. Trudeau was from Montreal and a true Canadiens fan. He thought that the hockey club had made a mistake in keeping Carey.

As the 2010 season was about to start, it looked like the angry fans were right. During Carey's first exhibition game he allowed 4 goals on just 9 shots. The fans were on their feet, booing. During the next game, Carey was struggling so much that the coach pulled him out halfway through the game. It looked like Carey's dream of being a top goalie in the NHL was fading. The pressure was starting to get to him. "Guys could go nuts playing net here," Carey told a sports reporter about being a Montreal Canadien. "It's definitely taxing mentally. You learn a lot of lessons in a place like this. You face a lot more pressure than other teams. But winning is the cure for everything."

Cool Down

After years of late-night hockey, Carey realized he needed time to relax and unwind. Playing games that stressed both his body and mind had turned him into a night owl. He'd be pretty pumped up when it came time for bed. Carey said to the *Globe and Mail* that he often couldn't get to sleep before three in the morning. Carey learned to do things to relax and he often played video games to try and chill out.

Carey was not giving up on his dream. But what could he do? All he could do was work hard to be the best goalie he could be. So, Carey went to work, determined to make the 2010–2011 season the best season of his career.

10 Tough Times for the Blue, White and Red

Carey was not just chasing his dream now. He had to work even harder to make his dreams come true. Carey was ready to prove to the fans and to himself that his best years in net were just beginning.

In the 2010–2011 season, Carey wanted Montreal to know they had made the right choice in keeping him. So Carey went to work in the net. He played like a true Number 1 goalie. He became better than ever. Carey said in a video interview that he loved to play at home: "There's nothing like playing in front of a crowd at the Bell Centre."

Carey had an outstanding regular season with the Canadiens and even set records in the league. He set a Canadiens record by playing 72 games in the season. It was the most games ever played in one season by a Montreal Canadiens goaltender. Carey had the most wins in the league and recorded his best GAA (2.35) and save percentage (.923). It was a personal best for Carey. He had 38 wins and was third in the league with eight shutouts. He was also picked again to play for the All-Star Team.

Carey helped lead the Canadiens into the first round of the NHL playoffs. Montreal played one of their oldest rivals, the Boston Bruins. The Canadiens won the first two games in Boston.

Carey stops to say hello and take a photo with a fan, December 22, 2009.

Carey was strong in net. But in Game 3 the series started to slip away from Montreal. They had trouble scoring.

And Carey was peppered with shots. He faced 51 shots in Game 5 and only 2 of them went in net. But Boston still won the game 2–1.

The series went all the way to a Game 7, winner take all. Unfortunately, the Bruins won the final game in overtime. Carey and the Canadiens were finished for another season.

The next hockey season, 2011–2012 was not very satisfying for Carey or the Canadiens. Carey's injuries resulted in a number of missed games. The team suffered without him in net. The Canadiens finished the season with a disappointing record of just 31 wins. Carey and the Canadiens failed to make the playoffs that year.

But, even with the team's losing season, Carey's abilities were still being awarded. He was asked to be in the All-Star Game for the third time in his career.

NHL All-Star Game

The NHL All-Star Game is an exhibition hockey event played by the league's stars. The players are chosen by fans who vote for their favourite heroes. Carey was selected by the Montreal fans. The All-Star Game does not count as part of the NHL standings. The competition is just for fun. The games feature a players' skills competition and a 60-minute game.

During 2012 Carey got to combine another one of his favourite pastimes, video gaming, with his love of hockey. *Assassin's Creed* video game developer Ubisoft asked Carey to help them launch their newest game, *Assassin's Creed III*. Carey agreed to help for two reasons. The company's plan was to raise money for charity, which Carey wanted to get involved with. The other reason was that the main character in the game, Connor, is half Native American and half English.

"It's not every day that a video game company comes to you," Carey said in an allhabs.net interview. "When I found out that Connor was half Native American, it touched me."

The 2012–2013 season was very tough for all hockey fans. The players and the owners of NHL teams were in a labour dispute. The sides had different opinions about how the game was being run. On September 15, 2012, the NHL team owners announced a lockout. The players were not allowed to play. Many people feared that there wouldn't be a hockey season at all that year. But an agreement was finally reached on January 6, 2013. The players, owners and fans were happy to have the game they loved back on the ice.

The season began on January 12, 2013. Carey and the Canadiens played well during the short regular season. They finished with the second-best record in the Eastern Conference and easily made it into the playoffs. Montreal played the Ottawa Senators in the first round. It was a close series until Game 4, when Carey was injured and had to leave the game. Carey didn't return to the series. The Canadiens lost the final two games. The Ottawa Senators won the first round and moved on in the playoffs. The season was over for Carey and the Canadiens.

11 Canada's Goalie

During Carey's incredible career he has had the honour of representing Canada on many different levels of hockey. His greatest honour came in 2014.

During the off-season of 2013 Carey had some big changes in his life, both on and off the ice. On August 24, 2013, Carey and Angela got married in Benton City, Washington, near the town were Angela grew up. They had been dating since they first met as teenagers.

Carey in net for Team Canada at the 2014 Olympic Games in Sochi, Russia.

On the ice, Carey was injury-free and playing well. The Canadiens were off to a great start to the 2013–2014 season. It looked like the Canadiens were going to be a strong team and make it into the playoffs again. Carey's great start to the season got the attention of another team too: Team Canada!

Before the NHL season got too far along, Carey was given a great honour by his country. Carey was chosen as one of three goalies to play for Team Canada at the Winter Olympics. The 2014 Olympics were being held in Sochi, Russia. Carey, Mike Smith of the Coyotes and Roberto Luongo of the Florida Panthers were named Canada's three goalies.

Shortly after the team arrived in Sochi, it was announced that Carey would be Canada's starting goalie. Team Canada's coach Mike Babcock had faith in Carey.

Carey knew he had one of the best teams in hockey playing in front of him. It gave him confidence in himself and his teammates. Carey's belief in himself would keep him in net for Team Canada for the entire Olympic series.

In the first game, Team Canada played Norway. Carey faced 19 shots and stopped 18 of them. Canada won the game 3–1. Carey continued to play hard during Game 2 against Finland. Carey allowed Team Finland to score just 1 goal. Canada won the game 2–1. In Canada's quarter-final game, Carey again allowed only 1 goal as Canada beat Latvia 2–1.

On February 21, 2014, Carey and Team Canada played the USA in the semi-finals. The two teams had been hockey rivals for many years. Carey stopped all 31 shots Team USA took on Canada's net. Carey earned a shutout in the 1–0 win. Canada's strong defencemen worked hard to protect Carey and the Canadian net. With Carey stopping almost every shot, the team was nearly impossible to beat.

Five minutes into the first period of the gold medal game against Sweden, Carey made a big save. Then Canada scored the first goal with seven minutes left in the period. By the second period, Canada had a 2–0 lead. Team Sweden fired a lot of shots at Carey, but they couldn't get one past him. In the third period, Team Sweden tried switching their lines around to see if they could get a goal, but they still couldn't score on Carey.

As the clock ticked down to end the game, Carey shut out Team Sweden. Canada won the game 3–0. They were Olympic gold medalists! As the players celebrated on the ice, Canadian fans everywhere were celebrating with them.

Keep Calm and Carey On

Lynda knew Carey was under a lot of pressure at the Olympics. He wanted to do well for his country. Just like when he played hockey in Montreal, Carey felt the stress of being in net. "I think the sense of connection to our land and where we come from helps keep us all grounded in who we are," Lynda said in a CBC interview. She felt that their culture had always kept Carey calm and connected to who he was.

Through the five-game series, Carey had an incredible save percentage of .972. He had back-to-back shutouts in the semi-final and final games. Carey allowed only 3 goals on the 106 shots taken on him. He was named the best goaltender at the Olympic Games by the International Ice Hockey Federation (IIHF).

Carey was thrilled to have his family with him in Russia at the Olympic Games. Many Canadian families made the trip with the team. One of Carey's biggest fans was in the crowd at the Sochi games — his mother Lynda. She had bought her plane ticket for Sochi as soon as she heard the announcement that Carey had made the team.

Carey was returning home with the award for best goaltender at the Winter Olympics. But that wasn't the prize that mattered the most to him. He and his teammates had won the gold medal! That was what really mattered. Carey said to the *Globe and Mail*, "I can't say enough about that team in front of me, that group of forwards and that defensive line. That was a real pleasure to play behind. There's no question, their work ethic was second to none this whole tournament."

It was an incredible Olympics for the Canadian Men's Hockey team. Before facing Canada in the semi-final and final game, both the United States and Sweden hadn't lost once. But Team Canada broke their undefeated records. Carey didn't allow a single goal in the last 164 minutes and 19 seconds of the final two games. CEO of the Edmonton Oilers and Former President of Hockey Canada Bob Nicholson remembers how important Carey was for Team Canada: "Carey Price was absolutely rock solid in goal for Team Canada on Russian soil in the 2014 Winter Olympic Games in Sochi, Russia. It was a true Canadian dominance led by Carey Price!"

After the six-day series in Russia, Carey and the team left to return home to Canada. They had their gold medals around their necks. "It sure is heavy. It's a really cool feeling . . . I'm really excited and honoured and grateful for this life experience," Carey told reporters.

Carey had become Canada's goalie. But for Carey there was more to being a champion than just winning gold. He had a lot more to prove. Not just to himself, but for kids who grew up dreaming just like him.

12 A Style All His Own

Carey was playing some of his best hockey when he returned to Montreal after the Olympics. Carey had earned a lot of fans all across the country after helping Team Canada win gold.

Back home to finish off the rest of NHL season, Carey was a force in the net. He had 34 wins by the end of the regular season play. His .927 save percentage was one of the highest in the league.

The Montreal Canadiens made it into

the Stanley Cup Playoffs again. Carey was in great shape. He had taken control of his position in the net. His combination of excellent reflexes and great reaction time made him tough to beat.

Bowhunting = Goaltending

Carey is an experienced hunter. This may be another reason he's so patient in net. To bowhunt you need patience and a good sense of timing. Goalies need to wait patiently for the shot on goal, then react quickly.

Carey had also perfected his style of blocking shots. From the time he was a boy, he had studied it, watching his goalie heroes. In the early years of the NHL goalies would stand up to block shots. Then goalies like Tony Esposito started to drop to their knees to stop the puck. In the 1980s Patrick Roy used the dropdown style and spread his arms and legs out wide.

It looked like a butterfly opening its wings. Carey and many other goalies began to use this style too. Carey could really fill the net with his butterfly position.

Carey also had his own special style when it came to his masks. Like all pro hockey goalie masks, Carey's are painted by artists with images the goalie has chosen. Carey's

The Anahim Lake town Welcome sign. Members of the Anahim Lake community gather to show their support for Carey and Team Canada.

masks have included cowboys, Team Canada logos, the Montreal Canadiens logo and *Assassin's Creed III* artwork. David Arrigo is the artist that does the paintings on Carey's masks. In 2011, Carey asked David to create a special mask to honour his ancestry. The mask had images of Anahim Lake, an Aboriginal elder and a dream catcher.

Mask Man

Carey helped design three different goalie masks. Fans could vote for their favourite design on TSN.ca. The winning design was made into 31 masks, to match the number on Carey's jersey. The 31 masks were auctioned off to raise money for different charities. The highest bidders got a chance to meet Carey in person.

In the first round of the 2014 playoffs the Canadiens faced the Tampa Bay Lightning. Carey and the Canadiens swept the series. They won the first four games and did not allow Tampa Bay a single win!

While Carey and the Canadiens were getting ready to face the Boston Bruins, the people of Anahim Lake held a rally for Carey. Carey had remained close to his friends and family back home. Carey went home every summer when his hockey season ended. Everyone in Anahim Lake came out to show their support for their hometown hero. The rally was held on the town's outdoor rink. They were excited that Carey and the Canadiens were getting closer to their chance to play for the Stanley Cup. If they won, the people of Anahim Lake knew Carey would bring the cup home for them to see.

Playing the Boston Bruins, the competition got a lot harder for the Canadiens. Boston went ahead in the series three games to two. Carcy had to work hard to protect his net. He let in only one goal in the next two games against the Bruins. The Canadiens won the series and moved on to the Eastern Conference Finals.

Just one more series win and the Canadiens would be playing in the Stanley Cup Final. They just had to beat the New York Rangers to get there. In the first game the Rangers took a 2–0 lead early in the first period. During the second period, the Rangers' Chris Kreider got the puck and took off down the ice on a breakaway. He sped toward Carey and the Montreal net. The Canadiens on the ice skated after him. But it was too late. Kreider crashed into Carey, smashing his leg into the goal post. Carey tried to keep playing but his leg was badly injured. He wasn't able to play any more games in the series. The New York Rangers defeated the Montreal Canadiens four games to two. The season was over for the Canadiens. Many hockey fans thought that if Carey had not been injured, the Montreal Canadiens would have won the Stanley Cup.

Carey's Personal Style

In an online video interview for the Habs, Carey joked about his sense of fashion. "I'm a small town western kid at heart," he explained. Carey still loves to wear his cowboy boots and hat. But he says that his fashion style has gotten better since he moved to Montreal.

13 Giving Back

Carey's steady play and remarkable abilities had made him an NHL superstar. Many hockey experts said that Carey was the best player on the Montreal Canadiens. Even players and coaches from other teams could see his incredible talent as a goalkeeper.

Carey doesn't really like all the attention. He just wants to play the game. He just wants to stop as many pucks as he can and help his team get the win. When asked to compare himself with a superhero, Carey told an interviewer he was more like Peter Parker than a hero like Spider-Man. But Carey is a special kind of hero.

Carey knows how fortunate he is to have a career playing the game he's loved since childhood. He also knows that being a hockey hero doesn't just happen on the ice. For Carey, doing what he loves is a blessing. He has had so much in his life because of hockey and he wants to share his good fortune with others.

For a number of years Carey and Angela had been involved in helping youth in Carey's hometown of Anahim Lake and in their Montreal community. Carey and Angela didn't just give money to help out charities. They gave their time too.

First Carey sponsored a group that works to keep kids from dropping out of school. As part of the Stick with School program, Carey donated a pair of hockey tickets to each of the Montreal Canadiens 46 home games. A child and their mentor are chosen to be treated to a game night at the Bell Centre. It's a special night out for these hockey fans, who might not ever get to see a Canadiens game live if not for the program.

In the city of Montreal, Carey has become very involved with community events that the Montreal Canadiens have organized. Carey visits the children's hospital to meet young fans. He attends the Canadiens annual Blood Clinic and the Canadiens Radio Telethon. Carey has also supported the Carson Kolzig Foundation that helps families living with autism.

All of Carey's kind work in helping others didn't go unnoticed in the hockey community. The Montreal Canadiens decided to give him an award for his important role in helping others. Every year the Canadiens organization selects a player who has shown generosity in their commitment to charity work. On October 14, 2014, Carey was honoured with the Jean Beliveau trophy. In a short presentation at the Bell Centre before a Canadiens pre-season game against the Ottawa Senators, Carey received the trophy. It was presented to him by Elise Beliveau, the wife of the former Canadiens player the trophy was named for.

Carey was very honoured to receive the trophy. He told reporters, "My wife deserves her name on the trophy more than I do. She's really the catalyst behind a lot of the work." Carey also received a $25,000 donation from the Montreal Canadiens Children's Foundation to donate to a charity of his choice.

Every year Carey returns to his hometown to relax and enjoy the peacefulness of Anahim Lake. But in August of 2014, his usual trip to Anahim Lake was extra special. Carey and his wife Angela were there to make a very special announcement. Lynda Price and her mother, Carey's Atsoo, were there too.

On August 19, 2014, Carey's mother, Lynda Price, presented a photo of Team Canada to Anahim Lake school. Carey is wearing a traditional hat with the Canadiens logo on it.

The entire local community crowded into the Anahim Lake School gym to see their very own NHL superstar. Carey was thrilled to announce that he was going to be the First Nations Ambassador for the Breakfast Club of Canada. The program has brought more than 10,000 meals to kids in his hometown every year.

The celebration honoured Carey's ancestry too. There were speeches about his great-grandfather, Chief Domas Squinas, a Nuxalk from the Wolf Clan at Stuie. Nuxalk dancers and singers performed. Carey was presented with special gifts from the community. He received a traditional cedar hat that had the Montreal Canadiens logo painted on it.

When Carey was asked to make a speech, he spoke about how peaceful his life as a kid in Anahim Lake was. "I had a lot of good friends here," Carey said. "It was quiet, we fished in the creeks and rode horses. I'm proud to have grown up here."

Carey was asked what message he had for the kids in his hometown. "I've been in your shoes and I really just have one message for you," he said. "I know what it's like to grow up in a remote place. If you get an opportunity, make the most of it. It doesn't have to be hockey, just use your best qualities. Do your best and opportunities will materialize from there."

Carey and his family also knew how important it was to protect their culture and heritage. It meant a lot to Carey. His mother Lynda said that Carey was interested in trying to protect their First Nations language. "We would like to see what we can do to help protect our language and culture for future generations," Lynda explained in an interview with the cbc.ca reporter Allison Devereaux.

Even though Carey is a busy NHL player he takes time to reach out to those in need. He lends his support through his charity work whenever he can. Carey also has taken the time to personally contact those in need. He has written letters to people who were sick or had lost a loved one. Carey's words of support meant a lot to those who received them.

In June 2015, Carey wrote a letter to Jason Coonishish, of Mistissini, Quebec. Carey had read about Jason's son and brother being killed in a hunting tragedy. They were with three other men who died when the hunting cabin they were staying in burned to the ground. Carey sent a card from himself and the team to let Jason know they were thinking of him. Jason was a Montreal Canadiens fan and his son, Chiiwetin, was a goalie. Jason told CBC News the letter Carey sent greatly touched him.

The National Aboriginal Hockey Championships

The National Aboriginal Hockey Championships are held every year. These hockey games are for Indigenous male and female youth in Canada. The teams compete for the National Championship crown. The tournament also includes coaching and skill development, cultural activities and a closing ceremony for the athletes.

14 A Fan Favourite

The 2014–2015 season was when Carey proved himself. Many sports writers said his 2015 year in the net showed he was one of the best goalies in the history of the game. During the regular season Carey posted a 44-16-6 record. In the 66 games he played, his goals against average was 1.96 and his save percentage was .933.

Carey had also become a very important leader on the Montreal team. Many of his teammates looked to Carey for hockey advice. Rule 6.1 in the NHL rule book says, "No playing coach or playing manager or goalkeeper shall be permitted to act as captain or alternate captain." So Carey couldn't officially wear the letter "C" or "A" on his jersey. But many still considered him a leader in the dressing room. Then Canadiens' coach Michel Therrien made sure Carey was involved in all the captains' meetings the team had.

Accomplishments on and off the ice had earned Carey many fans. Even if people weren't Montreal Canadiens fans, they still appreciated his great talent in the net. Some of the toughest hockey reporters in the world of sports had become Carey Price fans.

In December 2015 Carey added two more awards to his trophy shelf. He was a clear favourite for the Lionel Conacher Award for the Canadian Press Male Athlete of the Year. Carey won the award with 53

Georges Vezina (born 1887, died 1926), a Montreal Canadiens goalie, was the first NHL player to have a trophy named after him.

percent of the votes from sports editors and broadcasters from across Canada. It was the first time a goalie had ever won the award.

Later in December it was announced that Carey had also won the *Toronto Star*'s Lou Marsh Award for Canadian Athlete of the Year. This award was extra special for Carey. "Being compared with athletes from other sports, it's unique for me," Carey said. "I'm very honoured. It's something I'll look back at the end of my athletic career and probably highlight one of these as the top." Carey also had another message for the aboriginal people of Canada. "It's definitely something to look up to, for sure," Carey said, during an NHL.com interview. "It's something that I hope for a lot of aboriginal communities to be able to see and say that these types of things are obtainable for their children. All it takes is a lot of dedication and hard work and luck."

The Hockey Hall of Fame

At the Hockey Hall of Fame in Toronto, Canada, Carey Price is one of the players visitors ask about most. Carey has been part of a number of exhibits at the HHOF. His sticks, masks and World Junior jerseys are on display there. You can even take a shot on Carey at the "Shoot Out" interactive game rink. Carey is also part of a very special exhibit called "The Changing Face of Hockey: Diversity in Our Game."

Carey was being recognized and honoured as one of the best Canadian goalies to have ever played the sport. He had become an international sports star, known for his skill on the ice and his kindness toward others. Carey was not only admired by his peers, but by hockey fans everywhere.

As the 2015–2016 season rolled along, Carey continued to keep his fans in mind. He wrote letters, made some surprise visits and even photobombed some unsuspecting fans. During a game between the Montreal

Cree kids from Waswanipi send a special message to Carey.

Canadiens and the New York Islanders, a young Canadiens fan named Justin got a selfie with Carey. Justin and his family were in New York City to watch the game when Justin decided to take a picture with his camera phone near the ice. As he posed for the selfie, Carey Price skated up behind him and photobombed the picture!

The new season looked good for the Canadiens. They beat the Toronto Maple Leafs 3–1 on October 7 in their first game of the regular season. The team continued

From the Hockey Hall of Fame in Toronto, Canada. This display features Carey's World Junior mask and stick, along with his 2014 Olympic jersey. The exhibit was part of the 2016 Little NHL (Native Hockey League) tournament held in Mississauga, Ontario.

on a winning streak. They played 9 games without suffering a loss. On October 27, their tenth regular season game, they lost to the Vancouver Canucks 5–1. But they had set a club record for the best start in the regular season. It looked like Carey and the Canadiens were off to a great season.

But the team soon began to suffer a lot of injuries. At the top of the injury list was Carey. As the early season moved into late October, Carey suffered a lower body injury in a 4–3 loss to the Edmonton Oilers. Carey missed the next 9 games and didn't return to his position in net until November 20. Shortly after rejoining his team on the ice, Carey reinjured himself in a game against the New York Rangers. The Canadiens won the game 5–1, but Carey was in pain and did not play the third period. This time Carey wasn't just hurt, he was badly injured. He had to take time off to recover. In April 2016, the Montreal Canadiens announced that Carey's injury involved serious ligament damage (MCL sprain) in his right knee and that he would not be returning to play in the 2015–2016 season.

As the hockey season continued, Canadiens players suffered more injuries. Many of the injuries were serious enough to keep players from returning to play for a number of games. The Canadiens were one of the hardest-hit teams in the NHL to suffer injuries during the season. By the second half of the season, the Canadiens had one of their worst losing records in their team's history. The Canadiens did not make the playoffs that year. It was the first time they'd missed the race for the Stanley Cup since 2012.

Many Canadiens fans felt bad that their team had started off the season so well but didn't make the playoffs. They weren't alone, though. Canadian hockey fans across the country were disappointed. No Canadian NHL teams made the playoffs that year!

15 World Cup Champion

Even though the previous season had not been what the Canadiens had hoped for, Carey was about to have a very special year. "It's been hard mentally," Carey said on Sportsnet.com. "This has been the most trying year of my career. I feel more tired now than I do when I play hockey. Watching, I don't know how fans do it, to be honest. It's hard to sit and watch and not be able to do anything about it. It's the hardest part about this process."

The World Cup of Hockey is an international tournament. World Cups have been played in 1996 and 2004. The United States won in 1996 and Canada won in 2004.

Baby On Board!

On May 6, 2016, Carey and Angela had a baby girl. They named her Liv Anniston Price. Carey and Angela were thrilled to be new parents. Carey Tweeted about how much he enjoyed spending time with his baby girl.

The 2016 World Cup of Hockey was being held in Toronto, Canada. Carey was ready to take on the world in net for Team Canada. All the games were to be played at the Air Canada Centre, home of the Toronto Maple Leafs. There were eight teams representing hockey nations from around the world. Some fans worried that Carey wasn't ready to play because of his previous injury. They thought he might reinjure himself and not be able to play for the Canadiens. But Carey was ready to go back to work. He wanted to play.

Carey was starting goalie for the exhibition game. It was his first start since the previous November, when he got the knee injury that caused him to miss the rest of the season with the Canadiens. In the exhibition game, Carey was playing well. He looked good in the net.

Team Canada faced the Czech Republic to start the tournament on September 17, 2016. Carey had a shutout, with Team Canada beating the Czech team 6–0. Carey was back!

After his first win in a World Cup of Hockey championship, Carey's play was awesome. In the five games he played in the series, Carey allowed only seven goals. He helped beat Team USA, Team Russia, Team Europe and the Czech Republic. His .957 save average helped Team Canada win the championship. Carey finished the tournament with a fantastic record in the net. His 5-0-0 record meant that he won 5 games, tied 0 and lost 0. It was a great performance between the pipes!

The final game of the tournament was Team Canada against Team Europe. As with all the games earlier in the series, the arena was filled with fans from across the country. Everyone was dressed in red and white. Thousands of Canadian flags were being waved in the crowd.

Carey made 32 saves during the game, only letting in 1 goal. Team Canada won the championship, beating Team Europe 2–1. Carey played an incredible game, proudly wearing his country's maple leaf on his jersey and his mask. This was the

16th time Carey had won playing for a national team. The last time he had lost a game wearing a Team Canada jersey had been in April 2005. In the decade between, Carey Price had truly become Canada's goalie.

Carey said that the players really worked together as a team. "This group really bonded right away," he said to Dave Stubbs of NHL.com. "Every championship team says that, but right from the start of camp, we all bought in. That was our motto."

As Carey left the arena he was filled with pride. His wife Angela and baby daughter Liv were with him. Carey had brought baby Liv onto the ice and skated around with her during the team celebration. His team had played like champions for their country and they had won it all! Carey was the Number 1 goalie in Canada.

The Highest Paid Goalie in the NHL

In July 2017, Carey signed an eight-year deal with the Montreal Canadiens. Carey and the Habs made more hockey history together. Carey's new deal was worth $84 million. He would be paid $10.5 million a year to protect the net for the Canadiens. The deal made Carey the highest-paid goaltender in the NHL.

16 Remembering Where He Comes From

In March 2015, Carey and the organizers of the Breakfast Club of Canada put together a very special meeting. An 11-year-old boy from Anahim Lake named Trent Leon was chosen to meet his idol, Carey Price. Trent flew by plane, for the first time in his life, to Montreal, Quebec. He'd never seen a big city before. He phoned his grandmother when he arrived and told her the city "was hard to describe."

Trent Leon Meets his Hero

Trent Leon got to meet Carey Price in Montreal on March 26, 2015. His Anahim Lake School Principal Dylan Walsh asked him about his experience.

Q: "How did you feel when you learned that you were going to Montreal to meet Carey?"

A: "I was very happy."

Q: "What did you think when you first saw Carey?"

A: "I was very shy."

Q: "Did you really score on him 5 times! How did that feel?"

A: "I think so! It felt great!"

Q: "Did Carey give you any advice?"

A: "He told me to follow my dreams."

The next day Trent got his chance to meet Carey in person at the Canadiens training centre. As they sat in the dressing room, Carey gave Trent a Habs jersey and some other souvenirs. Trent gave Carey some gifts he brought from home.

Then Trent got to go on the ice with Carey and take a few shots at him. Later Trent surprised Carey with cards written by the children of Anahim Lake school. The cards were filled with good wishes and thank-you notes. Carey got very emotional as he read the cards. Global News reported that Carey had tears in his eyes when he said to Trent, "Thanks, buddy, that means a lot to me."

In the fall of 2015 Carey decided to help out kids in northern British Columbia. He was looking for a way to support young hockey players who wanted to play hockey just like he did as kid. Carey got together with CCM, a hockey equipment company, and bought $10,000 of gear. Carey purchased skates, sticks, helmets and goalie pads. Then he arranged a special delivery to the Williams Lake Minor Hockey Association he had played for between the ages of 9 and 15.

Carey's dad Jerry helped put the surprise donation together. Jerry said that Carey didn't want any kid to miss out on the chance to play hockey because of a lack of equipment. "He wants to make sure that people, and kids especially, know that he hasn't forgotten and hasn't just elevated himself to the point where he doesn't have time for the people who matter most to him," Jerry told a Global News reporter.

After every hockey season, fans look forward to the annual NHL awards. The 2015 awards were held in Las Vegas, Nevada, on June 24, 2015. That evening, Carey Price had one of the best nights of

This bench was created by artist Marina Papais, woodworker Daniel Collett and the students of Anahim Lake School to honour Carey and his commitment to the school and his hometown. It sits in the front hall of the school.

his hockey career. But Carey wasn't on the ice. He was scoring big at the NHL awards. By the time the night was over Carey had won four major awards.

That night Carey took home the Hart Trophy for the most valuable player in the

A glass star is featured near the Canadian goalie on the tribute bench. It symbolizes Carey's success. It is made of mirrored glass so students can look into it and see themselves working hard to be successful like Carey.

NHL. He was awarded the Vezina Trophy as the top goalie of the season and the Ted Lindsay Award for the most outstanding player in the league. Carey also shared the William M. Jennings Trophy, with Corey Crawford of the Chicago Blackhawks, for allowing the fewest goals during the regular season.

On one of the biggest nights in Carey's life, he chose to take a moment to encourage others. In a speech, Carey had a message for the First Nations kids who were growing up just like he did. He was quite emotional as he spoke about his life as a Native boy from a small town. He talked about how it took lots of hard work and dedication to make his dreams of playing hockey come true.

Proud of His Heritage

Carey received his official First Nations Status in 2011. His mother had always urged him to be a role model for Indigenous kids. It was important for Carey to have his Native heritage recognized. His mother Lynda, his Atsoo and his community back home in Anahim Lake were very proud of him.

At the end of Carey's speech, after thanking his teammates and coaches, Carey said, "I would like to take a moment to

These three Anahim Lake School students all got to travel to Montreal and meet Carey, as part of the Breakfast Club of Canada program. From left to right: Trent went in 2015, Kane visited in 2016 and Chrissie went in 2017. Carey is the First Nations ambassador of the club.

encourage First Nations youth. People would say it's very improbable that I'd make it to this point in my life. I made it here because I wasn't discouraged. I worked hard to get here, took advantage of every opportunity that I had. And I would really like to encourage First Nations youth to be leaders in their communities. Be proud of your heritage, and don't be discouraged from the improbable."

Carey ended his speech by saying "Sunachailya," which means "thank you" in Dakelh, the language of the Ulkatcho people.

Glossary

Amateur: A player who is not being paid to play a sport.

Angler: A person who fishes with a rod, line and hook.

Billet: To offer the use of a private family home for a player or student, to live in temporarily while playing or studying away from home.

Blue line: The lines dividing centre ice (the neutral zone) from the attacking or defending zones.

Conference Divisions: The National Hockey League is made up of 31 hockey teams. The league divides these teams into two conferences, the Eastern Conference and the Western Conference. Each conference is separated into two more divisions. This helps the league manage the teams playing schedule by dividing the season up into different divisions.

Defencemen: Two players who play in front of the goalie to help keep the opposing team from getting shots on the net.

Draft: A selection process of choosing players to become members of a sports organization.

Dream Catcher: A round-framed net, crafted with feathers and beads, used by some Indigenous cultures. It is believed to stop bad dreams and catch good ones.

Farm Team: Is a team for younger players to play on, while they train and learn to improve their skills. With this experience they move up to a higher within their hockey club.

Goal crease: The area in front of the goal line, often shaped in a semi-circle and painted blue.

Goals Against Average: A mathematical formula used to measure the number of shots a goaltender lets in.

House League Hockey: A hockey league where all the players belong to the same organization.

Lariat: A long light rope, usually made of leather or hemp, used to catch cattle or livestock.

Lockout: A time when owners stop players from coming to work on their teams. The owners do not pay the players and there are no hockey games played.

MCL Strain: MCL is the short form for Medial Collateral Ligament, an inner ligament strain.

MVP: Most Valuable Player — an award given to the best player on the ice.

Off season: The time of year when players aren't playing.

Overtime: Extended time of play after the full regular time has ended in a tie. The first team to score in overtime wins.

Reserve: A portion of land that has been set aside for use by Indigeous people.

Rookie: A player in their first year.

Save percentage: A mathematical way of measuring the number of shots a goalie stops.

Shinny: (Also known as Pick-up hockey or Pond hockey.) Generally a more fun or relaxed version of a hockey game. Often played with very little equipment needed, no strict rules, no raising the puck and all levels of skaters are welcomed.

Shootout: A series of shots taken on a goaltender at the end of a regular game that has ended in a tie, with no overtime winner. An equal number of shots are taken by both teams to decide a winner.

Shutout: When a team doesn't score at all during a game.

Stanley Cup: The trophy awarded at the end of the NHL playoff season to the championship team.

Carey Price's Career Highlights

Carey's Firsts

- First NHL Game – October 10, 2007 against Pittsburgh Penguins
- First NHL Win – October 10, 2007 against Pittsburg Penguins, 3-2 victory
- First NHL Career Point – February 9, 2008, an assist – in a 6-1 loss to the Ottawa Senators
- First NHL Shutout – February 16, 2008 against Philadelphia Flyers, 1-0 at the Bell Centre
- First NHL Playoff Start – April 10, 2008, against the Boston Bruins, 4-1
- First Playoff Shutout – April 15, 2008, against the Boston Bruins, 1-0
- First NHL All-Star Game – January 25, 2009, in goal for the Eastern Conference team

- First Molson Cup Player of the Year – April 14, 2009 for the Canadiens
- First NHL Goaltender to win the Ted Lindsey, Jennings, Vezina and Hart trophies all in the same season – 2015
- First NHL Goalie to win his first 10 games of the season – November 12, 2016, 5-0 win over the Detroit Red Wings

Medals

- 2004 – World Under-17 Hockey Challenge, St. John's, Newfoundland (Silver Medal)
- 2005 – Ivan Hlinka Memorial Under-18 Jr. World Cup, Czech Republic/ Slovakia (Silver Medal)
- 2005 – IIHF Under-18 World Championship, Czech Republic (Gold Medal)
- 2007 – IIHF Junior World

Championship, Sweden (Gold Medal)
- 2014 – Olympic Winter Games, Sochi, Russia (Gold Medal)
- 2016 – World Cup of Hockey Toronto, Canada (Gold Medal)

Awards

- 2007 – CHL Goaltender of the Year Award, Calder Cup, Tournament MVP 2007 World Junior Ice Hockey Championships
- 2014 – Jean Beliveau Trophy, Best Goaltender at 2014 Sochi Olympics
- 2014-2015 – William M. Jennings Trophy (Shared with Corey Crawford of the Chicago Blackhawks)
- 2015 – Lou Marsh Award – (Canada's Top Athlete, voted on by journalists)
- 2015 – Lionel Conacher Award (selected by the sports writers of the

Canadian Press)

- 2015 – Hart Trophy, William M. Jennings Trophy, Vezina Trophy, Ted Lindsay Award
- 2016 – Indspire Award (National Aboriginal Achievement Awards)

NHL All-Star Team:

- 2008 – All-Star Rookie Team
- 2009 – Montreal, Quebec / NHL Young Stars Team
- 2011 – Raleigh, North Carolina
- 2012 – Ottawa, Ontario
- 2015 – Columbus, Ohio
- 2016 – Nashville, Tennessee
- 2017 – Los Angeles, California

Three-Star Awards:

- Rookie of the Month 2007-08 March

- Monthly Three Stars
  2010-11 November (2nd)
  2014-15 February (2nd)
  2015-16 October (2nd)

- Weekly Three Stars
  2009-10 Nov 23 (2nd)
  2010-11 Nov 15 (1st)
  2010-11 Mar 7 (3rd)
  2011-12 Oct 31 (1st)
  2011-12 Nov 21 (1st)
  2013-14 Feb 10 (1st)
  2014-15 Nov 17 (2nd)
  2014-15 Jan 5 (3rd)
  2014-15 Feb 2 (1st)
  2015-16 Oct 19 (1st)
  2016-17 Mar 6 (3rd)

Acknowledgements

Writing a book never involves just the author. It's a team effort, much like a successful sports team. There are many people who worked alongside me, my teammates who helped bring Carey Price's story to these pages.

Firstly, I would like to thank my publisher, James Lorimer, for entrusting this book to me. I am sincerely grateful for the support of all the staff at Lorimer, especially Laura Cook and Sara D'Agostino. Most importantly, I want to thank my editor, Kat Mototsune, for her guidance, patience and friendship — I couldn't have done it without her.

I am indebted to the following people who shared their knowledge and history of Carey Price with me: from Anahim Lake School, Dylan Walsh, principal; Dianne Chamberlain, school secretary; Janie Jack,

Culture and language Teacher; and the students; Izak Westgate from the Hockey Hall of Fame; Bob Nicholson, the CEO of the Edmonton Oilers; Lorna Schultz Nicholson, Bill Hamade, Dave Stubbs, Ashley Isherhoff and the Community of Waswanipi, Kathleen Adams from Tri-City Americans and Kathy Smith from the Williams Lake Minor Hockey Association.

Although I was not able to interview Carey Price for this book, I would like to express my gratitude to the news, sports, and media outlets that have chronicled Carey's life and career. The following were invaluable resources for my research: canadiens.com, sportsnet.ca, montrealgazette.com, nhl.com, tsn.ca, cbc. ca, ctvnews.ca, allhabs.net, thehockeynews. com, hockeysfuture.com, canoe.com, theglobeandmail.com, kamloopsthisweek. com, habseyeontheprize.com, nytimes. com, and the Hockey Hall of Fame.

On a personal note, I want to thank my family who have supported my writing career in so many ways over the years — my daughter Nella, who has read over numerous manuscripts for me, my sons and my husband, George, my tech-support and number one fan. A big thanks to the Number 9 Writers' Group, who are a constant source of creative motivation. Thanks also go out to my friends and colleagues at the Toronto Public Library for their help and encouragement.

Finally, thank you to Carey Price. You followed your dreams and have inspired so many young people to follow theirs. You are more than just a hockey hero.

Photo Credits

Adams, Kathleen courtesy of the Tri-City Americans: p. 40, p. 42, p. 45, p. 47, p. 49, p. 50, back cover

Alamy: cover

Chamberlain, Dianne: p. 22, p. 25, p. 99, p. 108

courtesy of Aviation Unlimited: p. 34

courtesy of the Hockey Hall of Fame, Toronto, ON: p. 118

Hamade, Bill: p. 67, p. 68, p. 79, p. 114

Iserhoff, Ashley: p. 117

Nicholson, Lorna Schultz: p. 90

Madsen, Anita and Jim Balfe courtesy of Anahim Lake Resort: p. 12, cover

Pare, Sylvia courtesy of Dylan Walsh: p. 17

Smith, Kathy courtesy of the Williams Lake Minor Hockey Association: p. 33

Stubbs, Dave: p. 59, p. 84

Walsh, Dylan: p. 15, p. 131, p. 132, p. 134

Index